Mole
A small tunnelling mammal of Eurasia and North America.

Mouse
A small rodent with pointed snout and long tail.

Noddy
A gull-like seabird that nests on tropical coasts.

Oryx
A large rapier-horned African antelope. Some species of oryx are now greatly reduced in number.

Ostrich
The largest living bird, found in the drylands of Africa.

Panda, Giant
An endangered animal, native to China, that feeds only on bamboo.

Quail
A tailless plump gamebird found worldwide.

Quetzal
A forest bird of Central America famed for its magnificent tail plumes.

Rattlesnake
A venomous snake of the Americas.

Roadrunner
A ground cuckoo of the American drylands that eats insects and small rattlesnakes.

Skunk
A nocturnal mammal of the Americas famed for its unpleasant scent.

Tiger
Found in Asia, this greatest of all cats is now rare.

Umbrella bird
A large tropical bird with a black umbrella-like crest and long feathered wattle on its throat.

Viper
A venomous snake of Europe, Asia and Africa.

Vole
A small rodent with a short tail.

Whale
An aquatic mammal living in all oceans, now threatened by overhunting.

X-ray fish
A fast-moving, shallow water, tropical fish found in Venezuela, Guyana and the lower Amazon.

Yak
A large long-haired ox that lives in the highlands of Central Asia.

Zebra
Striped horse-like animal of open grasslands of Africa.

Some of the world's best known and some of the not so well
known animals are shown in this entertaining alphabet book. But
many of these creatures are in serious danger of extinction – the
giant panda, the tiger and the blue whale to mention just a few.
   We must care for and protect the world's animals – for their
sake and for our own survival and well-being. No one is ever too
young or too old to learn about protecting the world's wildlife.

British Library Cataloguing in Publication Data
Dorfman, Gillian
   World wildlife animal alphabet book.
   1. English language—Alphabet—Juvenile literature
   2. Animals—Pictorial works—Juvenile literature
   I. Title   II. Price, David
   421'.1   PE1155
   ISBN 0-7214-9532-X

First edition
Published by Ladybird Books Ltd Loughborough Leicestershire UK
Ladybird Books Inc Lewiston Maine 04240 USA

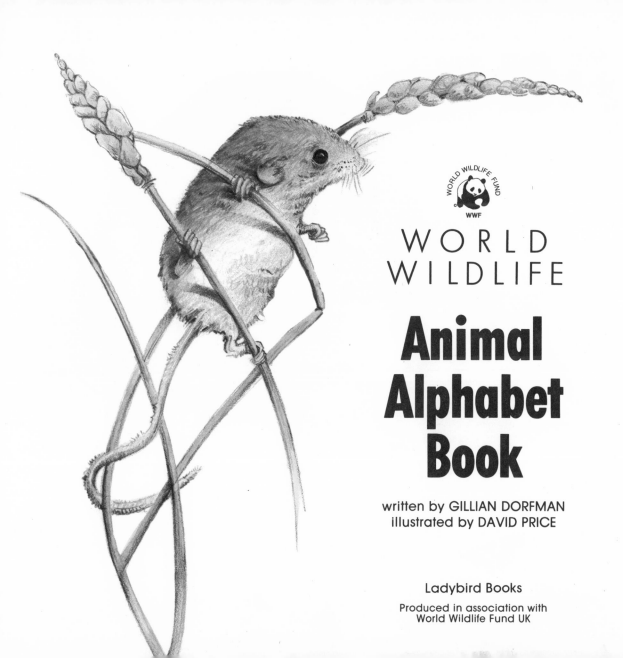

WORLD WILDLIFE FUND

WWF

WORLD WILDLIFE

Animal Alphabet Book

written by GILLIAN DORFMAN
illustrated by DAVID PRICE

Ladybird Books

Produced in association with
World Wildlife Fund UK

Aa

"Are you an ant?"
   an anteater asks an ant.

"Yes, I am. I'm as ant as an ant can be."

And so the anteater eats the ant.

Bb

dig!
dig!
dig!

"My beak is big,"
   boasts the bluebird.
"I can eat big beetles."

"My beak is bigger,"
   boasts the blackbird.
"I can eat bigger beetles."

But as the birds boast, the beetle burrows.

Cc

"Cougar, can you climb cliffs?"

"Of course I can.
I'm a cat, and cats have claws.
So I can climb cliffs.
And I can creep up and catch you.
So take care!"

Dd

"Don't we look dandy?"
  demand the drakes.

"You *do* look dandy," declares the duck.
"What a display! I don't know which
  I desire most."

So the duck dilly-dallies.

Exactly who lays eggs?
Eagles lay eggs.
Egrets lay eggs.
But elephants never ever lay eggs.

Ff

If a fish had fine feathers,
   could he fly?
Could he fly far and free
   like a falcon?
Fancy! That's just fancy.
A fish has fins! A fish can't fly.

Gg

"Giraffe, do you eat grass?"
   asks the gnu.

"No, I gather green leaves from trees."

"Good," says the gnu. "I'm glad."

And the gnus and gazelles graze on the
   green grass.

Hh

"Hyena, do you hiss, or hoot, or hum?"
  asks the hippo.

"I do not hiss, or hoot, or hum.
  I howl. Hear me."

And as the hyena hunts,
  he howls hysterically.

Ii

"Iguana, are you an insect?"
  asks the ibis.

"Insults! Insults!" says the iguana.
"I *eat* insects."

A jerboa jumps.
Is she jumping for joy?
No, she just jumps.
"It's just the job," jokes the jerboa.
"It's jollier than jogging!"

Kk

"Koala, keep clear,"
   says the kind kangaroo.
"I can kick. I can kill.
I'm not kidding.
But could I do karate?"

Ll

"Look, Louse, look!"
  says the leech.
"Look, I have no legs. I am legless."

"I have lots of little legs,"
  says the louse.
"I like my lots of little legs a lot."

Mm

"Mole, Mole, you're mad!"
  moans the mouse.
"Must you make many more mounds?"

"I must, Mouse, I must.
I'm a miner and I mine in the mud.
So I must make my mounds."

Nn

Do noddies eat nuts?
No, that's nonsense.
Noddies eat fish.
Do noddies use nets to catch fish?
No, they never need nets.
Noddies nimbly nip up fish.

Oo

"I am an ostrich.
I'm an odd bird.
I can outrun an oryx.
But when I open my wings, I can't fly.
That's odd."

"Where are the plants, Panda?
Where are the plants you pull up
    with your paws?"

"I am puzzled," says the panda.
"I am puzzled, because
    my particular plants
    will soon be no more."

Pp

Qq

"Quetzal, why do you quiver and quake?"
   asks the quail.

"I quake because
People hunt me for my feathers of fine quality."

"How quaint!" quips the quail.

"Shh! Be quiet."

Rr

"Rattlesnake, why do you rattle your rings?"
  asks the roadrunner.

He regards the reptile with relish.

"I rattle my rings at you, Roadrunner,
because I'd rather you ran away."

Ss

"You stink, Skunk.
Why do you stink so?"

"I may smell, but I'm smart," smirks the skunk.
"My special smell keeps me safe."

And the skunk sprays his stench.

Tt

"Tell me, Trapper, tell me,
Why do you try to trap tigers?"

"I trap them for trophies to trade."

"But, Trapper, tigers are not tame.
There'll be trouble if you trick them.
Truly."

Uu

"I'm upset," says the umbrella bird.
"I'm not ugly.
Under my beak I have unusual feathers.
I'm not ugly. I am unique."

Vamoose, Vole, vamoose.
Vanish before the viper gets you.
Vanish before you are the victim
   of the viper's venom.
But the warning is in vain.
The viper is victorious.

Ww

"Whale, in the water, do you worry
about your weight?"

"No," says the whale. "I don't worry.
I'm well content."

"Whale, would you wish to be willowy,
like a wand?"

"No, I would not. My weight keeps me warm
in the water."

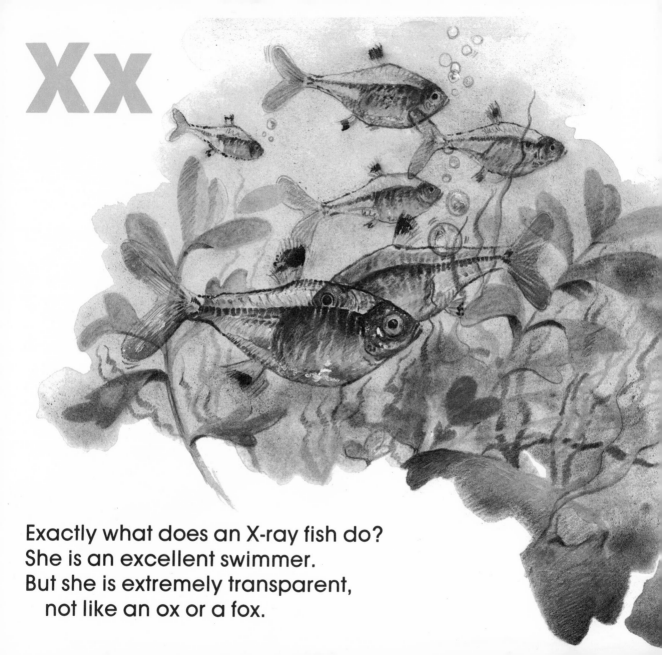

Xx

Exactly what does an X-ray fish do?
She is an excellent swimmer.
But she is extremely transparent,
　not like an ox or a fox.

Yy

"Are you a yak?"

"Yes, I am," yawns the yak.

"Are you a young yak?"

"Yes," yells the yak. "You *asked* me
  that yesterday."